Simple Truths

Being Prepared
A Practical Guide For Preconception

T0362780

GLOBAL
PUBLISHING
G R O U P

Global Publishing Group
Australia • New Zealand • Singapore • America • London

Simple Truths

Being Prepared
A Practical Guide For Preconception

Sandy B Simmons

First Edition 2014

National Library of Australia Cataloguing-in-Publication entry

Simmons, Sandy B., author.
Simple truths : being prepared, a practical guide for preconception /
Sandy B Simmons.

ISBN: 9781922118400 (paperback)

Conceptualism.
Concepts.
Perception.
Reality.

149.1

Published by Global Publishing Group
PO Box 517 Mt Evelyn, Victoria 3796 Australia
Email info@globalpublishinggroup.com.au
For further information about orders:
Phone: +61 3 9739 4686 or Fax +61 3 8648 6871

PRAISE FOR THE AUTHOR

"I recently had the pleasure of working with Sandy for a month at iLAB in Bali.

Sandy has great wisdom, an "elder" and with this wisdom comes a great capacity to listen.

Sandy is someone you can trust to help direct you in the way of being the best you can be. She will give you practical tools that will help to guide you to your desired outcome.

Sandy is an Inspirational Woman whose vision for the future is exciting."

All of us are leaving a legacy, Sandy is actively living her legacy and I am privileged to be part of her journey as she moves confidently into her wisdom.

Sallie-Ann Macklin *author of Inspirational Women – Ordinary Women doing the Extra-Ordinary, Founding Co-Director of Amazing People*

I first met Sandy many years ago when we both attended a year long training. I find Sandy to be rare as she is authentic and she really does walk her talk. In circles, she is renowned for her ability to synthesise her intuitive abilities with the wealth of her clinical experience. Her wisdom, expertise and care, never cease to amaze me as she facilitates others to achieve health, awareness, purpose and empowerment. I couldn't recommend Sandy highly enough as from my experience she is an inspiring mentor, consultant and teacher. Heartfelt thanks, Sandy, for your treasured assistance and finally for creating your magical legacy in print!

Lotus Rose, *Contemporary Fusion Artist – Designer,*
Founding Director of Deva Creations www.devacreations.com.au

DEDICATIONS

To my Dad, who lives on within me, being one of my biggest teachers

and

To all who follow their inner truth, to co-create heaven on earth.

REMEMBER, LESS IS MORE,
LOVE IS ALL THERE IS …

ACKNOWLEDGEMENTS

It has been a journey like no other, to conceive an idea, house it for a long period and transfer what's stored in the mind into a book, to endear others on like-minded journeys. It has been with much joy, mingled with a little trepidation, that I bring this topic to the fore.

A special thank you to my parents, Gwen and Denis, for my safe passage into the world and later passage to Australia. To my sister Denise, for her welcoming ear and who shares my life journey. To my adult children, Nicole and Steven for teaching me to laugh and keep moving, whatever the odds. To my partners for being who they are and contributing to my growth. I love you all dearly.

A heartfelt thanks to those who have looked after me, especially over the last year, including Greg. Thanks to my many friends and work colleagues for their support on many levels and who keep me grounded in everyday life. To Carmen, for her leap of faith in supporting me from the very beginning, Kirsty for providing the space to write, Duro for his significant insights, along with Roger and Paul for believing in my bigger picture.

Thank you to Darren Stephens who encouraged me to begin writing now, not later. For his unwavering inspiration and belief in my concept and the guidance and support of the team at Global Publishing Group.

To the many Mentors who have crossed my path and who are yet to arrive. I thank you all. Thank you for being who you are. I would not be who I am today if you had not passed by.

I am a rich reflection of you ALL!

FREE BONUSES!

Download your FREE bonuses NOW at

simplybetterhealth.com.au/simpletruths

*Something wonderful has transpired from your
purchase of this book.*

27 more children now have access to clean life-saving water.

Thank you.

Simply Better Health is a Proud Life Member of
Buy1Give1 – Business For Good.

TABLE OF CONTENTS

FOREWORD

In this world there has appeared a book, or rather a number of books – the combined works of an experienced naturopathic-nutritionist, who has seriously studied the issue of the correct preparation for what is entailed in bringing new lives into the world. This was especially written for the better half of humanity, womankind.

I have known the author, Sandy Simmons, for more than 15 years. She has helped many to achieve improved health by implementing innovative ideas with integrity and a genuine heart.

In these books, the author shares her vision of the psychological aspects of life, women's predestined role as life givers and how to approach conception, pregnancy and labour followed by the nurturing of a new human being in close connection with the mother's energy.

The main thread which can be traced like a red line throughout this author's work is how, by preparing and entering into full harmony with nature, a woman can gift to the world a new life that will also be harmonious and ultimately improve the collective consciousness of all humanity.

I have no doubt that many people who are going to read this work will enhance themselves as individuals and will look in a new way at many aspects of life, the value of which is difficult to overestimate.

This work contains a great deal of valuable and helpful material, especially for first-time mothers. You are holding a beautiful philosophical and practical guidebook in your hands.

Have a good journey!

Dr. Vagif Soultanov
B. Chemical Engineering; PhD Organic Chemistry and Chemistry of Wood; PhD Bio-chemistry; MD (Physician) Russia

INTRODUCTION

Do you ever stop to think about what life on planet earth is all about, how it is designed, why it manifests the way it does and what it means to be a human being?

Do you ever wonder about your own replication and the reproduction of the next generation?

You might wonder why I would bother to write a series of books on topics that are seemingly already exhausted.

For much of my life I have been an observer, witnessing over and over again, an endless repetition of themes passed down the human tree. Branches that loom over each human head, clouding thoughts and feelings, crowding the space within, causing confusion in knowing the self and appearing to sabotage glorious health and a heaven-sent human life.

I write and speak to inspire and re-educate about self-responsibility towards natural vitality. The secret lies within each human being, to hear individual truth, and regain the freedom to live a beautiful life. A life full of 'ah-ha' moments, filled with joy and passion, sadness and grief - the full spectrum of being human.

Would you consider living the simple truth of who you are, enabling yourself to experience your own freedom, so that your offspring are free to be who they truly are?

What would it take for you to believe that there are endless opportunities and possibilities for you to nurture yourself and the next generation? It's in your hands. What will you do?

IT'S ALL ABOUT YOU, YOUR STORY AND HOW YOU INFLUENCE THE WORLD!

The old saying 'know thyself' is very appropriate here.

Being authentic, more present, forgiving and able to receive, will support you on your journey to give the next generation the seed to worthiness, to experience their life of freedom, contributing to their next generation and beyond...

Enjoy your journey, may it take many twists and turns, create wonderful experiences to understand yourself and in so doing, continually let go of that which no longer serves you.

❧ ❧ ❧

The "BEING" series of 5 books called Simple Truths is designed to promote thinking past the current status quo of health issues for our future generations. In this first book we discuss 'Being Prepared,' A Practical Guide to Preconception.

Being Prepared for Preconception is often not in our consciousness, so this book is designed to bring your thinking around to see how you create your own life, mostly subconsciously. It gives you the space to see what is possible and why it is beneficial to explore your own beliefs and get to know your own self intimately before creating another human being.

There are platforms in place to facilitate movement into clearing your mind, cleaning your body, reuniting with intuition, strengthening the self and giving rise to a life free of past dogma. Then, when challenges present themselves, we are aligned with ourselves and have the ability to flow rather than resist.

Bonus offers are available from the website including further information, audio and videos, worksheets and booking a private consultation. This book contains links to access this information.

Being Prepared is designed to provide insight into four areas that are vital to the journey of pregnancy and parenthood:

- Restoring health – a peaceful mind and a vital body.
- Reducing health issues that have been handed down the family tree.
- Healthier offspring and a more harmonious life for all.
- The possibility of pregnancy when it seems impossible…

> *You are a significant drop in the ocean and simultaneously, you are the ocean.*

> *Do not let the future be held hostage by the past.*
>
> Neal A Maxwell

Chapter 1

✺

STORIES
and even older stories
called MYTHS

Mind Clear

Would you love to be clear in your head, know what your life is really about and be able to make the very best decisions for yourself, so that your life impacts favourably not only on yourself but also those you cherish? And more importantly, on those who have not been birthed yet.

Perhaps this possibility would be what most humans aspire to, or is that just an assumption?

Welcome to your inner and outer worlds. Do you know which one is running your life?

Are we are talking here about the original chicken, before the egg was even thought of?

What you believe, as prospective parents, grandparents, siblings, aunts, uncles, cousins, friends and acquaintances, is ultimately what you think. Do you have anyone in your life at this very moment who is considering conceiving a child of the future and contributing to the population of our world? Maybe it's you? Perhaps it will all go smoothly. You may wonder whether it will happen straight away or whether there may be a few hindrances and if so, how long it will take. Perhaps you have family members or friends who are a couple living together. Perhaps someone you know has opted to be a single parent. Maybe you know a same sex couple and you're wondering how it will happen for them. How do you know what to believe and what is actually possible? Are any judgements starting to rear their ugly heads?

What you think will colour your emotional response.

I invite you to come on a journey to explore and understand your human inner world!

Here we're going to touch on thoughts, feelings, perceptions, assumptions and beliefs and how they inform your choices. Whilst all these components are part of what we need in order to see the world in the individual way that we do, the essential point is how we put them all together. Yes, this is how you create your life.

First There Was A Thought!

So, let's look at 'a thought.' Where does it come from and what does it do?

Many thoughts flow through our body, moving on vibrational waves, from the outside in and inside out. There is much scientific information suggesting that the brain processes 400 billion bits of information per second but we are only aware of some 2000 of these. So, it follows that a single concentrated bit of information is a possible thought.

Even if it was less than 400 billion bits of information, that's a huge amount for our brain to compute and our mind to filter and don't forget the bank of information already housed inside our mind. Where did all that come from? It appears as if the brain doesn't know the difference between the information it receives from the inside or the outside world, as our brain reacts to both in the same way. Not only are we bombarded from the outside but we are also crowded from the inside with information that may have been handed down to us along with what we have made up since we arrived on planet earth! Wow, what a jam packed mind we house? What do we actually absorb? "Mmmm…" I can hear you saying, 'Perhaps this is why I'm often confused?'

As our thoughts, our memory and the outer incoming information that we gather through our five senses (sight, sound, touch, smell and taste) are aligned, this attraction of thought-memory-information creates our reality. Has this got you thinking?

Over thinking, under-thinking, just thinking… sometimes gets us somewhere and at other times it doesn't. What really matters is that it takes an enormous amount of energy to think and it can create a mountain of stress.

Let's have a look at creating a place to allow your mind to rest. Let's take the first essential step to understanding what thoughts do. This is a little exercise you may like to try.

Getting comfortable is vital, whether lying down or sitting, it doesn't matter. Just find a space to be on your own. Close your eyes and take three full breaths and let out your biggest sigh each time you breathe out. Let all the surrounding sounds recede into the background and allow all your thoughts to flow past. Notice that your thoughts are no longer penetrating your being, they are just out there floating by. Breathe in and out three more times, keeping your eyes closed. See if you can notice a sensation somewhere in your body. Perhaps you may have a nagging sore area. Place your left hand over the area where you feel uncomfortable, it will help to keep you connected to this place. If you get distracted, just re-feel and explore it for at least 10 minutes. Now open your eyes and consider what you have just experienced.

When you connected to that area of your body, did you laugh or cry? What came into your mind? If you would like to write the experience down, write while it's still fresh in your mind. What counts here is connecting to the feeling. I call this 'the space within the space' where you begin to connect to 'your true self,' your inner compass. You can do this anytime, anywhere.

In resting the mind and allowing thoughts to recede, we begin to understand that feelings run deep within us and realise that maybe those feelings could be colouring our daily lives.

BONUS

AUDIO MEDITATION –
CONNECTION

simplybetterhealth.com.au/simpletruths

We recognise our feelings when we feel happy or sad or we feel healthy or unwell. A feeling is attached to the memory of what we previously experienced in our life. The other day I was feeling sad after I called a friend who didn't answer their phone. My thoughts went to a childhood experience where I was feeling sad about being left out of a friend's birthday party. I made up a story that she didn't like me. Now when this friend didn't answer the phone, my thoughts repeatedly told me, 'She doesn't like you!'

Does this sound familiar to you? How instantaneously this happens within us all. My perception was totally different from my friend's perception of the event. I found out later that she was just not available to pick up the phone but I assumed she didn't like me. The reality of the very new friend's 6th birthday party was that I had only just moved to the school the previous week and the family didn't invite me as they didn't know I was there, which could begin another story! I'm sure you all have just as many tales to tell!

By now you may be realising how thoughts and feelings together initiate how we see the outside world and produce our perceptions! Assumptions are made up from what we think, feel and perceive so that it makes sense to us and helps us to justify our existence, just as I assumed that my friend didn't like me because of a previous thought and feeling experience colouring my perception and giving me a false assumption. We live like this every day. It takes us into a place that is not really comfortable and uses our time, consuming and exhausting our energy.

Now we have explored thoughts, feelings, perceptions and assumptions. Put all of these together and you have our beliefs. Notice, I said our beliefs! Think about the beliefs we have taken on from those around us, our family, work colleagues and friends. Not only do we have our beliefs, we took on others' beliefs as we grew, which clouds the belief system that we operate from. It's little wonder that we don't understand ourselves! The longer we live and stay this way, the more we forget who we are. Unless, we stop and reassess, recreate and grow, our lives will go around in circles for ever more, repeating the same old, same old and passing it on...

So from this point on, what will you do? What choices will you make?

Choice is consistent with our own underlying belief system of assumptions, perceptions, feelings and thoughts. You know, those decisions you make moment by moment, the ones you are mostly subconsciously making and unaware of. It's like when you drive the car and you wonder how on earth you got from A to B or the automation of getting off the train and going straight to the office or knowing how to make a cup of tea. But wait! You also know you have the ability to choose with awareness, don't you? After all, our choices create our reality, don't they?

Choices are a wonderful opportunity to take us wherever we would love to be!

I trust you can see a glimmer of hope to move beyond the status quo?

Let's move on and explore stories. We all have them. Who would we be without them? Would we be who we are today if we didn't have a story? And if we add the stories and myths of old to our story … what do we get? Let's look at this another way…

Imagine that we are in a world where there are no choices to make, our stories are all the same and where we are all doing the same thing. Now, where would that lead us? Wouldn't we be a replication of what has gone before and become robotic, continuing the same old status quo? What if our earth decided not to evolve any longer? It would stagnate. It may no longer revolve or even be involved in the universe. Where would that leave you, an inhabitant of planet earth? Do you think you may end up a little stuck?

How lucky are we to have the ability to choose? We are able to decide what we would love in every single moment of life. It's what makes every living thing different and unique. It gives us the diversity of nature and infinite possibilities. Our world continues to evolve, revolve and be involved.

Have you ever thought about the hundredth generation syndrome? It is my idea of explaining how much information we must have stored from many generations before. I'm talking here about the endless repetition of themes passed on down the human tree. We have handed down to us all that has gone before. It's in our DNA, our memory banks are full before we are even birthed. What if we let go of what doesn't serve us in our present lives? We would be lighter and so would our offspring. What a wonderful start to a new life that would be! Can we go back in time and start again? No, but we can clear our mental pathways, be lighter and unburden the next generation, allowing them to be liberated at the very beginning of life so that they can evolve into their unique self more easily.

Why do we bother to make choices about our self-reproduction? Doesn't procreation just happen? It's just random and chaotic anyway, perhaps a bit of a gamble. When a sperm is lucky it is greeted by an egg, sets up a romance and there you have it, or not! Who are we to interfere with nature, what difference does it make?

By now you may be starting to understand why, at times, it's so complicated to choose. You may have an inkling that both your inner world and outer influences are often in conflict and dictate the choices you make. It all depends on what information you are fed and whether it is truthful or just a myth.

Before your physical existence you were pure creative spirit with the intention of experiencing and expressing yourself as a human being. As you became this seed in thought, you were vibrationally matched to a male and female human, who were ripe for conceiving. Upon physical fertilisation, your spirit begins to unfold, your particles grow inside your mother's womb and when you are ready, you are then suddenly born into another world where you continue to grow outside of the womb and begin to navigate life on earth. You build on an ever growing bank of information with your perception of each individual experience, culminating in your own personal belief system. You know this is so, however, your sister, brother, friend or foe may perceive the same experience differently and in varying degrees from you. So, who is right? There is no right or wrong. It's the conflict of perceptions that feeds thoughts and feelings that causes confusion.

Emotions are vibrations, they also colour your thoughts with feelings. What was going on while you were growing in the womb? Yes, even while growing as a foetus you are thinking and feeling! What emotional vibrations were you receiving?

Do you believe that what you think and feel together gives you the tendency to make well informed choices? Perhaps it's so coloured by your own experiences, it's clouded in judgement. What about the previous generation's experience? Where does that come in? What is it that you would love to pass on to a newborn human soul? So many questions, it's all too much! STOP!!!

Imagine if you don't know, how will the young people know? Are you willing to explore some personal issues to be prepared?

Let's get to the simple truth!

What we perceive and assume, we believe, think and feel, the total of which impacts on all those around us and is also housed in our very own mind, so is easy to pass on to the next generation to subconsciously replicate.

Really, we just need to be conscious of who we are as individuals! The old saying, 'know thyself' is very appropriate here. Listen within, to how you react and what makes you tick. You will hear when to stop repeating what has gone before. Let go of that which no longer serves you.

Then, our internal being becomes clear, imaginative and creative.

We support creating a beautiful mind when we nurture our spirit within. This flows on to the way we feel, perceive and choose, without assumptions and judgements... to be in life.

Add to this a well-rounded and balanced life in the physical world by walking, joining a martial arts class, a creative venture, a happy relationship and doing work that you love and much more...

ALL of these factors culminate in life experiences, helping you to become more authentic to yourself, which is then projected to the outside world.

Being authentic, more present, forgiving and able to receive, will support you on your journey to give the next generation the seed to worthiness, to experience their life of freedom, contributing to their next generation and beyond...

Once you have somewhat sorted and melded your own thoughts, feelings, perceptions and ultimate beliefs, what choices will you make? What stories will you change? Will you pave a new-found path? After all, we are all ultimately responsible for being who we are and what we project. What and who we are influences our society at large. Depending upon your new way of thinking and choices, you could contribute to the next generation being freer to evolve into who they truly are.

There are a multitude of reasons for preparing for conception as there are a multitude of ways you can be a parent. For example, you could be a dynamic couple who conceives straight away or has difficulty conceiving, you could be adopting, you could be a same sex couple, a single parent or you may decide to have donor eggs and sperm… Everyone wants the same outcome – to produce healthy offspring! To bring a new generation into being, free of the hereditary dogma of the past and participating in a vital future…

By now, I trust you are somewhat clearer as to the way our lives are formed, from thoughts to beliefs of both ourselves and others. We can observe and become aware of how we operate in the world and how we can change to contribute to a much brighter, vibrant, graceful and loving world…

And yes, you've got the idea, we make it all up!

So to keep your complex mind simple, we have crafted 5 key elements to create a vital peaceful mind of your own:

1. **Inner influence**, where does it come from? Inheritance – you can wallow in what has gone before or you can stand on the shoulders of giants to create something new.

2. **Outer influence**, where does it come from? Life experience – you can take on others' thought forms or you can look between moments for your own.

3. **Know your own beliefs** – ability to be non-assuming and non-judgemental.

4. **True choice making** – ability to keep outside influences at bay.

5. **Bliss** to be who you are in any one moment – <u>YOUR SIMPLE TRUTH.</u>

BONUS

WORKSHEET NUMBER 1

simplybetterhealth.com.au/simpletruths

> *From the dust of stars to the human form.*
>
> **Sandy B Simmons**

> *Insanity is doing the same thing,
> over and over again,
> but expecting different results.*
>
> **Anonymous**

Chapter 2

✺

SIGN POSTS
What to look for and who to listen to

Body Clean

Do you know when you don't feel ok? Do you listen to your body? It speaks to you in every single moment, feeding back information to let you know when it's happy, humming along or not feeling so great. If you don't know, how will your children know?

Do you listen to others about your own body? Do you really think that they know more about you than you do? Yes, there is always much to learn about ourselves; as humans we seem to have lost much of our individual knowing. Consulting a healer is often necessary to wake us up and get us back on track but do they know more than you, about you? Not really, we just need help to wake up and remember that our true inner guidance is priceless!

Certainly, prevention is much better than cure. Your spirit knows how to live and flourish within the body it has created. It is within you to know how to operate your body. This is great, but how do you know what to do, when the seemingly obvious is not obvious to you?

So what do you look for? Sign posts. Sign posts are all over our body, if only we could observe ourselves, we would see when we're 'not quite right.' If we have a nagging backache from lifting something too heavy, you know it will heal on its own with some rest but what about a backache that could be caused by inflamed intestines, would you recognise that? You may not be able to make that connection. You may not have been taught to recognise what can affect what! Oh, how blissfully unaware and out of touch we have become with our bodies, treating them like they're going to keep on starting up every morning, forever!

Those of us who drive a car know that our vehicle needs maintenance. If we didn't maintain our car, change the oil, clean it out, feed it what it needs, it will STOP!! Yes, STOP!! It just cannot go any further, it needs to rest, perhaps even be rebuilt or just be refuelled.

Do you STOP when your body asks you to? Would you recover more quickly if you did? OR do you soldier on and realise that there is nothing else to do but run on empty, thinking you have to do it all as you couldn't possibly stop?

Perhaps you've had a diagnosed health issue and you say to yourself, 'So this is it. I've got what my parents had. I must be getting old. I just have to live with it!' This is a sign post! Who says that you have to repeat a disease that has gone before? Doesn't that happen when something is out of control – YOUR control? What happens when you are diagnosed and 'boxed' by society with a particular issue and you are told that the only way out is to take some medication that will alleviate the symptoms? What, no return to vitality!! EVER!!

Our mind controls our body. When we are told that we have a certain disease, our mind says, 'Oh no. Now we're in for it! This is what happened to my friend and I've read all about it. It looks as if that will now happen to me,' and you get ready for the ride of your life. Do you know that when we use our inexperienced information, from reading or being told how to make a choice, we imitate that information, as we have not felt and integrated the experience to know the difference?

Our crazy collective belief systems, stories and myths about health are not serving us at all. They are actually destroying humanity. Do we really want to pass this on to the next generation? Where have all the sign posts gone?

Mostly, we are not listened to and that is reflected inside. We are all so busy with busy-ness, when do we stop to really listen to others, let alone ourselves? In our current medical system, you are 'in and out' in 10 minutes. If you get a script for medication, you think 'Ah that's great! Now I know I have something wrong with me. I feel cared for and now I have been given medication to take care of it.' Even with some of the more traditional medicines it's the same. You go home armed with many medications to help you deal with your situation. They may listen to you longer in their consultation but are you any the wiser as to how to recognise your e-motional sign posts and perhaps change your thoughts, beliefs and lifestyle? You've actually ignored your inner knowing and handed your power over to another human to give you some relief or to reinforce and justify that what you are doing is okay. Will you regain your health? Maybe, maybe not. The thing is, you listened to your sign post but you didn't know what to do. The answer was within you but you chose to ask someone else what you actually already knew.

Can you see that we all really need a shake-up, to wake up to recognise our very own sign posts?

ONE tool that I use is to 'un-rhyme your rhythm'… Disrupting your usual habits by taking steps like asking yourself, 'How can I be different in life?' Take a look at this video to understand more:

BONUS

**VIDEO –
RHYTHM**

simplybetterhealth.com.au/simpletruths

So, it's time to connect, re-evaluate and create a new story, a new way forward that will enhance humanity and create healthy offspring to live freely to be who they truly are, knowing when discomfort and ultimate dis-ease knocks at the door inside, that there is something to address before it becomes 'bigger than Ben Hur'.

One sign post for me throughout my life is that I have an extremely sensitive digestive system. If it doesn't want something it will automatically throw it out either end. Another common human sign post is when circulating blood deposits toxic residue around joints and other organs as it flows by. It may create issues such as skin rashes and organs that don't work efficiently. On investigation at an early stage, there appears to be nothing really wrong and you feel like you are stumped, with nowhere to go, as the test results say you're okay. This is the critical time to take note of your sign posts and listen to your inner being. You know it is time to do something about your health, but what? Sorting that out, as many of you know, may be a very lengthy process.

If you don't know, you don't do and if you don't do, you don't have to worry about it. This form of apathy is probably the most common form of denial on the planet. This is a sign post! What about the age old golden rule of 'know thyself'?

You are denying your own self nurturing, your very life existence. You are ignoring your inner self who knows how to look after you in all manner of forms.

What if we knew what to do for ourselves? How to nourish ourselves in every possible way. We cannot continue to blame anyone but ourselves! After all, we are responsible for our own health and behaviour!

So, let's look at where we are and the next steps to take…

You are heading in the direction of parenthood with a system that isn't working well internally. Do you feel that your body is healthy enough to procreate? Who would you actually create in this instance? Whether male or female, everyone requires maintenance in one form or another. With a little reflection on what's actually happening, you become clearer about what to do next.

We know that 'to do as I say and not as I do' just doesn't work! The new story is 'see what I do, see the benefit and do this with love for yourself.'

There are a multitude of ways to clean your body – find one that reso-nates with you. To allow your body to rest and recuperate, both inside and out, reflects the love that you have for yourself.

What do we mean by a clean body? Well, we can shower and bathe and that's great – a bit like washing the car on the outside – looks great, shiny and sparkly but what's lurking under the bonnet no-one really knows! We could put off a service – the car could stop tomorrow or it could go limping along for what seems like forever – or we can main-tain our 'pride and joy' with a regular service and have a happy purring vehicle. If you don't maintain your body, are you being apathetic or loving? I hear you say, what about 'time and money' – now is that just another story?

What is important to YOU? What message are you giving yourself, your family, the world…???

The story is strong in many people. The sign posts totally lost. How do we move past the status quo that has been handed down to us?

Another age old golden truth that needs to be known is 'Allow the process to unfold.' But what does that mean?

If you have a cold, what do you do? This is another sign post that you need to stop, keep warm and take nourishing warm foods and drinks and rest. If you take something to stop the cold from progressing, you stop the process and 'house' the energy of the cold inside your body. The cold has not been allowed to proceed. The cold happened for a reason. Your immune system went into action to remove dis-ease and would like you to rest so that this process can happen quickly and easily. This is your body talking to you and telling you what you need to do.

You're writing an article. You don't have a lot of time and you don't check it properly! A sign post perhaps. Slow down, there will be enough time to go through the process to get the end result you would really love, a great article with your name on it! It's the same with baking a cake, driving to an appointment and so on…

Let's introduce emotions into the story.

We are talking here about energy in motion (e-motion). So the processes that stay stuck inside become e-motions. These e-motions are your sign posts, they trigger thoughts and feelings and the same story goes around and around, UNLESS we decide to listen to ourself.

So now we have a clear mind and know what e-motions do. Are we ready to clean up our body? Do I hear a resounding YES?

The very decisive act of choosing to do this will attract your next step. You will know where to go for assistance, when to do it and then what to do will become obvious.

You may be female or male, getting ready to procreate or not. You may be looking forward to becoming grandparents, aunts, uncles, cousins or best friends. It is each and every individual human's responsibility to shower the next generation in an honest, authentic and genuinely truthful way. And there is no better way than to know who you are than by nourishing yourself as only you know how. This enables you to understand the new being that has arrived and allow them the freedom to experience their journey not bound by what has gone before.

Let's look at the simple truth of health.

While health appears to have become complex, it is actually quite simple. The choice is yours and always at your fingertips. This is not the place to get into a debate about nutrition but I do believe nutrition is not just about what we eat and drink. Whole nutrition encompasses relationships, environments, exercise, fresh air, deep breathing, colour, sound, doing what you love, being kind to yourself and much, much more. It's about nurturing yourself and others along the journey of experiencing life as a human being.

However, as nutrition is seen as largely about food, let's discuss it briefly. You've made a mindful decision to change your lifestyle. Your body loves and thrives on basic whole food, it loves to be nourished, sustained and cleaned by it! Whole foods are those that are in their natural state, directly after collection by harvesting. We eat and drink to sustain a balanced body by replenishing elements required for homoeostasis.

So, what do you do now that is not in alignment with sustaining a self-regulating vital body? What about your reproductive system, is it working well? What you ingest has a vibrational effect on your body. Do you always know what you are taking in?

We may grow our own or buy biodynamic /organic fruit, vegetables and grains, as many are now chemically sprayed and grown in soil depleted by farming through the ages. Much of our meat, fowl or fish are also contaminated in some way, shape or form. Free range, grass fed and chemical free proteins are often difficult to find. In our age, mass production + mass distribution = mass ingestion + massive waste.

Label reading becomes paramount as GM foods begin to creep into our everyday foods from all over the world.

Do you eat because you don't recognise thirst any more or because you are upset? We all know we don't think and feel so much when we're eating so it pushes that feeling or thought deeper inside! We eat because it tastes nice, yummy and sweet and our body just craves more - perhaps because it's just there, put in front of us and we're told when to eat, how much to eat and that we must eat everything on our plates. Does this ring any bells?

Addictions to sugar, to carbohydrates and so on… provide such great comfort! Alcohol and drugs are great for distorting our reality, taking us away into realms where we are numbed out, away from the present. Remember we are here to experience life, to allow life to make us feel, to alert us to change our ways and move into a higher potential! The first thing that happens when you change old habits is that you feel and you think, 'Oh no, this is too much, I can't do this.' Then you retreat and go back into the same old pattern.

Do you have children around you? If so, they are observing your habits and will add this repertoire into their very own belief systems!

We need to wake up. Wake up to ourselves and responsibly nurture our beautiful gift, our body. Yes, being human is a prized gift, not something to be dishonoured or thrown away.

Sign posts take a little time to notice. Check in with yourself and scan every part of your body with your eyes closed. Believe me you will notice exactly what isn't running well.

What you think, feel, assume, perceive and ultimately believe dictates both how you nourish yourself and how you live your life.

Many people come and go from our lives; we attract those we need at different stages throughout our life. Take heed of who you mingle with. Spend more time with those who help to nourish you. The way you are 'being' will then impact favourably on all those around you! Great relationships are as important as nourishing foods.

Your sign posts are real! You do know what to do. It is your responsibility to be a vital human being before the procreation process and to influence the next generation in profound ways, enabling them to have sovereignty of their life.

Summary – 5 golden rules to superb vitality

1. **Inner Influence** – You just don't feel quite right. Will you do anything about it? You can ignore it and allow it to grow inside or you can clean your pristine vehicle.

2. **Outer Influence** - You've got a rash all over, will you hibernate? It might just go away or you can explore options to clear it.

3. **Know your sign posts** - Listen to yourself, you know what to do next, you house everything you need.

4. **Believe in yourself** - Know that anything is possible and that possibilities are endless.

5. Bathing in the restoration of **YOUR SIMPLE TRUTH**.

BONUS

WORKSHEET
No 2

simplybetterhealth.com.au/simpletruths

We are organic bodies living in an organic world.

Sandy B Simmons

> *To live is the rarest thing in the world.*
> *Most people exist, that is all.*
>
> Oscar Wilde

Chapter 3

✹

INTUITION
The inward journey/clarification of self

Spirit Being

Of course, you know you have intuition, or do you?

Simply put, so far we have gathered a clear mind and a clean body. What comes next? Perhaps some further conscious awareness will take us to where we would love to go! So, what does being aware mean? In earlier chapters we explored being in touch with our mind and body and hearing what it has to say. That is about becoming inwardly aware. You know that gut feeling or 'sixth sense' that is often talked about? That is when our awareness is heightened. We are in tune with our highest potential and our intuition comes into play.

In order to prepare to be in awareness and conscious of what we are doing in as many moments as we choose, we need to be absolutely present. What does it mean to be present? We all have a past, present and future.

You can live in the past, repeating the same old patterns or you can be totally occupied by the future, thinking of how it will be and what you have to do OR you can choose to be PRESENT! Meaning that you are in neither the past nor the future but you are focused with your whole being on the HERE AND NOW!

This is an important aspect of life that has been hidden and not often handed down the ages to the majority of society, only to a select few in the world. It is so important as it underlies our whole existence. We undermine our very wholeness when we are distracted by the past or the future.

Can you imagine being born with your intuition intact? Actually, we all are. Take into consideration the story about life we have all entered into, the environment and how we have navigated our way through the first seven years. Most of us will have hidden our intuition because it seems that we are not in tune with our collective surroundings and we've decided to pop it to one side for the moment…

The story goes something like this. We imitate our family and peers to the 'nth degree' with what appears to be the best loving intentions in the world to nourish ourselves! We tell ourselves, 'Yes, this is definitely the way, the only way to live. It doesn't really feel quite right but hey, if I don't do it this way I won't fit in. I will be in trouble and, oh boy, that means that others are not going to be very happy.' This is how we adapt, making up how life is from our environment.

As we grow into our teenage years we may become rebellious as there is still enough intuition housed within us to know that what's going on is not always 'okay' and not really the 'truth.' A sign post perhaps? As we grow into adulthood, these thoughts and feelings come into play and we don't do anything about them. These are what we often call 'excuses' as adults and a really great sign post to give us the cue to look at how we are being in the world. This can be overwhelming and many will just put their heads in the sand and say, 'It's just too hard.' We tell ourselves, 'This life was okay for my parents and so this is how it is, it's okay, not too bad!' However, any honest adult will tell you that there is still a battle raging within. I'm sure we all have our own very tantalizing stories to tell. Some of them so great, that we seem to have moved through the most gruelling times and are still here to talk about it. We delight in sharing our comparisons on how life is so difficult, so hard. Does it really need to be? Could life be only as hard or perhaps as easy as we choose to make it?

Could there still be a little intuition left behind the mask to keep us in the truth of who we are? Is it becoming more transparent?

That spark of intuition, when we have a clear mind and a clean body, gets fully ignited and WOW, life starts to get REALLY exciting! Watch out world!!

We begin to feel differently about ourselves, we start to understand ourselves and realise what it feels like to be really alive. We start to have an inkling as to why we are here. We connect with our inner self and move easily on the path of least resistance, to remember and love our purpose and feel like we've 'come home.'

So, how do we know we have found our intuitive self?

There are a myriad of ways to recognise your intuition. Has someone ever appeared in your life just at the right time to help, work with or just be with you? This is when you attract what you need. For example, it is often said 'the teacher appears when the student is ready.' With awareness, we can access our intuition at any time we choose. We really just need to ask ourself, 'What do I love and what do I need to do next?' Much easier said than done, when we haven't been taught this or even seen it in action previously in our life.

ONE thing that I have found helps me is this exercise: As soon as I wake in the early morning, I sit quietly and comfortably, on my own, feeling refreshed, with a clear head and clean body. Closing my eyes, I allow all the sounds around me to recede into the background and move my attention to my body. I 'look around' my body to see if I feel uncomfortable anywhere. If I am, I move around and finally settle comfortably. I re-focus and feel deep inside into my secret space, that special spot I was in most of the time as a young child, in my innocence. Accessing my deep inner space, my intuitive self, I just know what is coming… just as you did when you were a child. For instance, I know that today I will write 2,500 words for my new book. Then, I know that I need to clear the space for this to happen. My day begins… I choose to follow this profound inner guidance.

BONUS

AUDIO REFLECTION – INNER SELF

simplybetterhealth.com.au/simpletruths

There is no doubt that there have been many times in your past when you have known what to do. You may have been unsure how you did but you felt the time was right or a job was right for you or you needed to say something 'now' and everything works out well. This is your intuition at work behind the scenes. For a split second you were right here, right now and it felt like you were riding on top of the world. However, we often lapse into unconsciousness as we move through our days and nights, oblivious of our own intuitive power.

How would it be if you could be fully conscious and access your intuition in an instant? Well, that's actually how it works. It doesn't have to be worked at, it's always there. It's just you remembering that it's there. Other humans and all living things can sense it in you but we are often so disconnected we 'can't see the forest for the trees.'

Another little story – in England, I was at Grammar School with all the trimmings and trappings that it entails. On arriving in Australia I went to a High School, one that had no uniform and very few rules. I found it very difficult to be present as I was swinging from Grammar School to High School, surely there was a happy medium, I was very rarely present – I was just coping with my new extreme.

Like the swing of the pendulum, how much swing are you experiencing? Where are you on the plane?

< Past	Present	Future >

Imagine looking at your hands. The left is the past and the right is the future. Your left is your known, your past - the right is your unknown, your future. What would happen if you brought them together, like praying?

This is when you are truly in the present – focused on the here and now. Duality has come together and we could even call it Oneness!

Let's just recap…

You are a drop in the ocean and the whole ocean at the same time. This is what we call duality. Being human, we are gifted with the choice to be this way or that, to experience life. Before we are born and when we die, we all go back into the whole ocean and become one. We are all parts of the One. The One cannot experience duality!

Your vibrations and your thoughts affect everything and everyone around you. How powerful are you?

Remember that your thoughts create feelings, create assumptions, create judgements and create beliefs and then you create your choices. Thoughts and feelings are attached to our memories. Assumptions and judgements come up as we know from previous experience what will happen. We believe this so deeply that we either react or do not react. This is what is going on moment by moment, every day in every way, month by month, year in year out…

What about choice? Yes, we always have choice. If we just stop and take a breath, mentally putting our hands together and seeing each situation as it really is here and now, then we will receive our own truth to see what to say or do next.

Can you now see that how you operate in this world profoundly affects the next generation?

We may constantly be going around in circles to fix what has gone before. Some areas of our lives are just not fixable and some are. When we intuitively understand that we just need to leave something alone and move on, it's a great sign post. We just need to stop trying to make it work.

You now know what it's like to have a clear head, clean body and access your intuition.

Do you still feel the need to wait and be given permission or approval that you are okay before you move on in life? Of course not, as you know you have everything within that you could possibly ever need. You now feel worthy and whole, like you 'belong,' you can trust, feel significant and you are capable and visible, with no need to control. You are totally transparent and genuine.

You have harnessed your intuition, your connection with spirit. Will you be part of the legacy for generations to come… allowing each one to be who they truly are?

As we acknowledge our intuition and know it is accessible at any one moment in time, we live the life we love. This keeps us in our truth, reflects this reality back to others and teaches the observers how to live authentically.

Summary – 5 ways to harness your intuition

1. **Inner Influence** – Your inner self houses all you need, you know who you are.

2. **Outer Influence** – Outside permission and approval no longer required.

3. **Know your intuition** – Bring the past and future together to be PRESENT.

4. **Access your truth** – Moment by moment with authenticity, no hidden agendas.

5. **Living** transparently – **YOUR SIMPLE TRUTH.**

BONUS

WORKSHEET
No 3

simplybetterhealth.com.au/simpletruths

Losing it all, gaining myself.
Sandy B Simmons

> *By being yourself,*
> *you put something wonderful*
> *in the world*
> *that was not there before."*
>
> **Edwin Elliot**

Chapter 4

❦

ACTION

Implementation and follow through – true to self

Ready Steady Go

You know there is a tomorrow and many great things will come, but how and when? This is one of the great questions of our time. How do we bring forth what we would love?

We just need to be who we really are and state not only what we would love but why!

Let's look at how we are travelling... So far, we've cleared our mind, we've cleaned our body and we've connected to our intuition. What next?

Our journey so far has taken us from an e-motion to a belief and everything in between. Then, we journeyed through our body discovering sign posts and now believe that we do know what to do next. Having a clearer picture of ourself and a cleaner body, we then discovered that our intuition has always been intact, since birth and perhaps earlier.

So here you are, ready to bring it all together. That includes both prospective parents. It's also inclusive of everyone connected with babies and children. I would say that would be the majority of the planet. You are a part of the collective consciousness, creating a new way forward.

I would like to add at this point, that changing thought processes and beliefs is not something that happens overnight. It's time for you to be patient with yourself. I would suggest at least one week for every year since your birth. Somewhere between 26 and 39 weeks, that is six to nine months, will give you time to integrate and implement a new way of being.

When we are discussing physical health, this is so obviously tied up with our thoughts and beliefs. It is often noted that small issues may right themselves naturally within a short time. However, if you have deeply imbedded acute health issues, the natural view of recovery suggests one month for every year you have accumulated the dis-ease.

I believe that every living body has the capacity to renourish and regenerate their health to regain the freedom to live to their individual highest potential.

I'll share this true story with you. I began wearing glasses from seven years old, as I could not see the blackboard at school. Every year my lenses were increased in strength. I thought it was wonderful each time I received a new pair of glasses. I could see so clearly, way beyond anything I had ever seen before. However, by the time I was 10, I was wearing glasses full time. I really needed to, as every time I looked up to see what was going on, the scene before me became hazier and blurrier. One day, in my teens, around 15, I remember taking my glasses off and not wearing them for some weeks. I couldn't recognise anyone on the other side of the street, nor see the blackboard at school. However, I'd had all the jokes to contend with, '4 eyes' and all that jazz, and I was just rebelling, as many teenagers do. I wasn't comfortable or happy at all. So, I ended up wearing my glasses again as I couldn't continue to function in life without them. They were a crutch I couldn't let go of. Contact lenses came into being and saved my life from ridicule and life became more bearable but it was still a significant nuisance and I lacked confidence and they limited my ability to be involved in activities such as swimming. I could never find anyone at the beach when I came out of the water. I couldn't look after my sister, who is 10 years my junior, at the swimming pool. She had to look out for me.

In the ensuing years, I went to a few opticians and asked them to reduce my lenses. I was feeling very uncomfortable inside, especially on the left side of my body, even to the point of feeling somewhat screwed up, stressed and quite irritated about life. I found that the general optician would not come to the party because on checking my sight with reduced lenses, I couldn't read the letters required for standard vision. I was becoming more and more frustrated.

Let's move on some 45 years from the beginning of wearing glasses at age seven. I had tried many different health-rejuvenating ways to regain better eyesight, none significant enough to alleviate wearing glasses. A few patients told me of a new optical system in country Victoria and said that this new way was working for them. So, after hearing about this three times (my sign post to take action) I finally made an appointment to see what was different and if it was for me. On the very first visit, my myopic lens prescription decreased considerably, from -5.5 to -3.75 and I was so relieved. I felt so comfortable inside, I was ecstatic and I could see better than I had for many years. And so, my journey over the last few years has culminated in only having to use a very small lens prescription. I now only wear my glasses occasionally, such as when driving in the early morning and evening when natural light is subdued. Old habits die hard. I often go to touch my glasses and I don't have them on. I have a great chuckle when this happens, at the wonder of the living proof of immense reversal of my eyesight. There really are no words to describe this feeling.

So, what is it that you aspire to? What we are talking about here is inspiring each other to be the very best human being we can be. When we radiate a balanced mind and vital health it is reflected out to others, allowing them to see what is possible, giving them the vision of possibility in their own life. Your 'little observers' will have a completely different perspective on life.

Now, let's take this a step further and talk about implementing. We've discussed how long it takes to change our beliefs, so how best do we go about this?

Remember – You have all that you need.

You may be recognising some of the dead wood you would like to decrease from your mind; some beliefs that are really not serving you anymore. They're actually taking up space and becoming a real hindrance. By now you may realise that your thoughts create your reality - those powerful inner thoughts that often scream at you. They've been there so long and built up to a crescendo. Meditating or writing will lower the decibels of the scream and allow the space for connection to self, to hear the whisper of your intuition and ultimately allow it to take precedence.

Work on one belief at a time and give yourself the time you need. It may be for one day or one week. Many of you may take more time. It all depends on how long this belief has been around and how strong it is.

BONUS

VIDEO –
CREATING CHANGE

simplybetterhealth.com.au/simpletruths

Let go, as per meditation in Chapter 1. Feel the feeling, go through the process and allow it to unfold. Going through the process is important, as remnants which are somewhat suppressed and unable to be completely expressed will stay inside and return, although to a much lesser degree. When complete, you may choose a ceremonial closure and lay it to rest OR you may realise that this belief is actually serving you and you discover that it's not as ugly a thing as you thought it was!

You may simultaneously be working on a new choice that you would like to bring into being. Here you may initiate and follow through the process. Writing the new belief down helps to cement it into your beliefs, reflecting back to your mind that this is what you would love. Acknowledge the commitment to yourself here.

Declutter to become clear. Removing the chaos in your physical environment will reflect back to your mind that you are following through with your choice and being true to yourself. This is your new reality.

Over the months you will be happier as you draw closer to how you like to show up in the world, with a vital mind, radiating abundant health and ready for whatever comes your way.

So now it's action time. You're really in the swing of knowing yourself and your partner or close friend and vice versa. Life is transforming in front of your eyes and you encourage and reflect being at your highest potential.

You will find the people you resonate with, who are walking a similar path to you. You will understand your family more. You love them dearly and always will but there is a time when you establish your own values and beliefs that serve you as you grow and transform.

This is what we call growing up, adulthood, perhaps we could also call it enlightenment.

There are many parents who are still acting out their childhood or teenage story. They have not moved beyond it. When they produce their offspring, the children observe this behaviour and do not know that growth in the mind and spirit is essential to a human being's journey of contentment and peace.

Is this starting to make sense? Of course, we all revert backwards and forwards, into and out of our stories, which is part of being human. The difference is that you are aware of what you are playing out and have the ability to self-correct and take responsibility.

Respect for ourself, our partner and our children is paramount for family harmony. We need to listen to each other. We need to listen to our children, they are often our biggest teachers, reflecting back that which is not working (sign post here) giving us the cue to reflect and rethink what we are portraying.

Let's look at what is primarily important in life.

If I were to ask you to leave your home, perhaps there's a bush fire coming… what would you take with you? It's imminent and there's not much time, literally minutes, what is most important to you?

Whatever you take with you will be a fraction of what you had materially but you will still have the whole you! Is this called 'lightening the load?'

Here's another story to demonstrate. I am reminded of my Dad when I realised that he, and I'm sure there are many others, migrated to another land to leave behind what he wanted to forget and move on from. My dear Dad left behind his material possessions but still had the same thoughts, feelings and memories intact – they came along with him. Life was not that different, perhaps a little worse and the cycles of the past repeated themselves again and again. Did he lighten his load? No, his belief system was so strong that he wasn't prepared or able to let go of how he thought life had to be. Dad has been amongst my biggest teachers.

As parents and guardians of the next generation, we will always be behind them. As much as we endeavour to grow our spirit and change our behaviour, children will learn from us, perhaps what they don't want in their lives. This is a natural process. It goes both ways. We also need to listen and learn from the incoming souls. Knowing your spiritual, inner self is a part of life. If it's ignored or not known, how much harder life will be. Giving a clear and clean platform for the next generation to start from, allowing them to stand on your shoulders and see much further than you ever will – that is evolution at work.

Summary – 5 ways to action your new way of being

1. **Inner Influence** – Process change within.

2. **Outer Influence** – See past the status quo.

3. **Know your action steps** – Change a belief - 1 day or 1 week.

4. **Access yourself** – Intuitive knowing.

5. There's nothing to do but action to take – **YOUR SIMPLE TRUTH**.

WORKSHEET
No 4

simplybetterhealth.com.au/simpletruths

Extracting Simplicity from Complexity.

Oscar Wilde

There are only two ways to live your life. One is as though nothing is a miracle. The other is as though everything is a miracle.

Albert Einstein

Chapter 5

❦

BLISS
Enjoy the journey

Soul Shines

Are you really on a journey and if so, to where?

Look at how far you have come in your life, what has transpired on your journey over the last four chapters? Know there are endless possibilities of creation that are available to you.

Why have I taken you on this journey? It's really quite simple, it is wise to know yourself before you create and/or guide another human, so that you can nurture that new being as nature intended.

Earlier we spoke of sitting on the top of the pendulum and watching it swing or being on the end of the swing. Which takes up the most energy? Which one is wise?

To be human is to experience duality. When we are unbalanced we know we need to address something and change what we are doing.

You are a contributor by being who you are, whether you realise it or not. You contribute whatever you portray toward our collective humanity, consciously or subconsciously.

What is your legacy to pass onto your offspring and the children of the world?

The old proverb **_'To know and not do, is not to know'_** is a reminder to take action (a sign post). It's time to move beyond wherever you have been before. You now know that you attract what you think and believe and you always get what you need.

As you know, life is often unpredictable and plans do not always come to fruition. Sometimes you plan and fail and sometimes you are pleasantly surprised. Learning to ride the waves that arrive at the most opportune or inopportune times and your ability to stay standing and be okay with what has transpired, is a mark of respect for who you have become.

Inwardly, you are lighter, have inner strength, feel very different and know more of who you are and that you are able to live life in harmony whenever you choose.

Outwardly, you are now prepared to discern the truth from whatever comes your way. You are being a part of humanity and all there is!

There is no separation, just an individual experience of being human. When you are a spirit without a body, you can only experience the pureness of being one. However, you are here right now, present, with your own beliefs intact, your intuition to guide you, bringing forth your wisdom. How blissful is that!

So, where does unconditional being and love fit in? Well, it's the tip of the iceberg.

Unconditional love is to 'love in all conditions.' We really don't need others to change for us to maintain our own wellness. If we step in and take over another's life, believing we are helping, it's a sign post for us to change the way we perceive another's journey. We don't need to rescue them, we need to love, support and encourage them to overcome their own challenges. When loving unconditionally we see the very best in each person, their shining light, even if it's only a spark. We can then hold ourselves in our highest vibration and shift into our own shining light, allowing our greatest gift to flow and elevate those we love, which reflects back on ourselves. Then we are able to hold the space of non-judgement for ourselves and others, relieving the stress of having to be that which we are not.

Continuing on our journey to self-discovery…

There are as many options as there are beliefs. You may have come through a transformation to realise that perhaps you do not want to physically have children to contribute what you would love in the world. There is no right and no wrong. We are all guardians for the next generation, in all manner of forms. It only matters that you choose what you would love. It may not be what is expected but knowing your 'why' liberates both yourself and those around you.

But what if you know that your 'why' is to head into the physical birthing of a new soul?

Well, preparation for consciously conceiving is paramount, especially in our current times, where we are full to the brim with the past… more so than at any other time in humanity's history. There is a recognition and need to let go of what does not serve us as individuals, to allow the space to create what we would love.

When I'm asked what is a good amount of time to prepare for pregnancy, I would say six months at least, preferably nine. There is much to reflect on, realise, take action on and implement in daily life – yes, great personal and lifestyle changes are afoot and your contribution to the next generation is imminent.

There are practical aspects to look at for both males and females. Know your hereditary predispositions and address any health issues you currently have. The healthier you are, the healthier your offspring will be and in turn, life will present in ways that you never thought possible.

For men, it is suggested that having a comprehensive health check, including a sperm analysis, reveals empowering information for yourself and your partner.

For women, it is suggested that having a comprehensive health check and keeping a thorough menstrual cycle diary from now on gives you an instant overview, also revealing and empowering yourself and your partner.

Another aspect to consider, if you are taking the oral contraceptive pill, is to change to reproductive-friendly products such as sperm-friendly condoms and vaginal lubricants, allowing your body to come back to its natural cycle.

Perhaps you are taking medication, either medically prescribed or self-prescribed. You may consider having this checked and reviewed.

Overall nutrition is part of what being prepared and taking self-responsibility is all about.

So now that you have somewhat sorted and melded your own thoughts, feelings, perceptions and ultimate beliefs, what choices will you make? And, what stories will you change? Will you pave a new-found path? After all, we are all ultimately responsible for being who we are and what we project. What and who we are, influences our society at large. Dependent upon your new way of thinking and choices, you could contribute to the next generation being free to evolve into who they truly are.

You will thank yourself for taking time to prepare and for getting to know your inner self and the way you tick, so that you can bring to fruition only that which you would love to accompany you on your own journey to fulfil your senses and purpose while living on this beautiful planet we call earth.

Whether you choose to physically give birth or not, adopt or be a carer for a child, when you grow through self-responsibility on all levels, it will create a different platform for our young people to springboard from, a place of endless possibility.

Summary – 5 ways to enjoy the next part of your journey

1. **Inner Influence** – Reflect on what you would love.

2. **Outer Influence** – What do you portray to others?

3. **Know your Journey** – Why do I need to change?

4. **Access your bliss** – Know contentment and joy.

5. Live – **YOUR SIMPLE TRUTH**.

BONUS

WORKSHEET
No 5

simplybetterhealth.com.au/simpletruths

> *Make a Difference – Live Heaven on Earth.*
>
> **Sandy B Simmons**

AUTHOR'S FINAL WORD

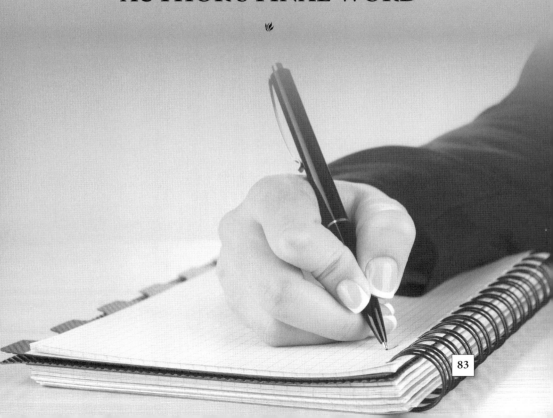

Thank you for choosing to read 'Being Prepared,' A Practical Guide for Preconception. I trust you have found the treasure you were looking for to enable you to move past your current state of mind, body and spirit.

Here at Simply Better Health we are happy to hear from you and help you in any way that will benefit you and your future family - email us at simpletruths@simplybetterhealth.com.au to find out your next steps.

I look forward to sharing the next part of your journey in my next book –

SIMPLE TRUTHS
Essential Beliefs

A Practical Guide for Conception

Mums' Connection
Supporting Mums Globally

THE MUMS' MOVEMENT

The Mums' Movement has been created to walk with you through the time in your family's life when you are considering procreating through to the first 9 months of your baby's new life. Born from an idea that community spirit runs deep within us all, with the common thread of world-wide motherhood, we are able to support each new life birthed and their carers. *The Mums' Movement* is a platform for learning, sharing and celebrating a new way forward for our next generation.

Taking time to prepare for the arrival of your new baby is wise. We are here to walk alongside you with guidance, support and information, celebrating milestones with you over the next 2 years and 3 months and beyond.

BONUS

JOIN *'The Mums' Movement'* NOW

simplybetterhealth.com.au/simpletruths

ABOUT THE AUTHOR

EDUCATOR, SPEAKER, INTERNATIONAL AUTHOR

An Entrepreneur, leading Naturopathic Nutritionist and International Author, Sandy B Simmons is the Founder and Creator of Simply Better Health.

Upholding her vision for each human to know who they truly are in being a part of the whole, Sandy gathers the conscious collective to initiate the journey into a sustainable world. She consults and speaks to our global community to create simply better ways forward.

A change maker, Sandy shares her expansive knowledge alongside her ancient wisdom, encouraging humanity to ride the waves of diversity, creating vitality within and without our ever changing life on earth.

Sandy's mission is to shine light, enabling regeneration towards global health for the next generation and beyond through the catalysts of education, self-responsibility, environmental preservation and innovative strategies.

Sandy B Simmons has travelled a personal and professional journey that has taught her how to nurture the seeds of change in herself and others. Author, educator, practitioner and speaker, Sandy uses her unique talents to inspire compassionate awareness and loving-kindness in everyone her message reaches.

Born in London, England, Sandy immigrated to Melbourne, Australia at the age of twelve. Having been exposed early in her life to children from many cultural backgrounds, she approached each new development in her life with a wise openness. She earned the nickname, "Miss Independence," from family and friends because of her adventurous nature.

Sandy's perspective on life can be summed up in her quote, "Don't let anyone tell you that you have to live a limited life. Be unique and choose the freedom of living your truest purpose and greatest potential."

True to her beliefs, Sandy has led an extraordinary life of growing, working, learning and loving. The path of her life is intertwined with constant exploration, self-study and training in an eclectic assortment of fields. To improve her own family's health and wellbeing, Sandy learned about general nutrition and breastfeeding. Later, her studies turned to natural nutrition and fertility and many supportive modalities. While enjoying a healthy lifestyle, she travelled to Alice Springs, Australia, to study colour, sound and breath work.

Sandy has been fortunate to discover many mentors and experience many life changing modalities. Her life changed forever after a near death experience and she began to focus her energy on educating and empowering others to not only improve their health but also increase their overall sense of wellbeing.

Simply Better Health is Sandy's platform for consulting and mentoring. She offers a range of services designed to assist her clients with mastering themselves and connecting with their true nature and purpose. Her services include nutrition, natural fertility and lactation consulting.

She also provides transformational coaching which involves one-on-one readings and supportive mentoring that empower her clients by helping them align their passions and purpose with their life choices.

It's obvious to everyone who meets her, that Sandy embodies all of the positive characteristics of her birth sign – Sagittarius. She effortlessly combines her optimism, confidence, enthusiasm, frankness and spirituality with boundless generosity.

Sandy is the author of Simple Truths – *Being Prepared – A Practical Guide to Preconception* and the creator of the BEING book series.

Sandy's professional affiliations include the Australian Traditional Medicine Society, International Institute for Complementary Therapists,

Nutrition Australia, the Australian Breastfeeding Association, the Lactation Consultants of Australia and New Zealand, the International Lactation Consultant Association and the International Baby Food Action Network (IBFAN).

Adventurous at heart, Sandy is a world traveller. Her quests have taken her to places that include Italy, Spain, France, Belgium, Holland, Liechtenstein, Germany, Austria, Singapore, Indonesia, Abu Dhabi, Oman, Kuala Lumpur, India, Croatia, Switzerland and Luxembourg.

Sandy lives in Melbourne, Australia.

RESURCES

Other Books by the Author – Coming Soon

Being Prepared - A Practical Guide to Preconception is the first in the 'BEING' series of Simple Truths –

1. Preconception

2. Conception

3. Pregnancy

4. Birthing

5. Lactation

FURTHER READING

Biogenealogy: Freedom from the Ancestral Origins of Disease by Patrick Obissier

The Biology of Belief: Unleashing the Power of Consciousness Matter and Miracle by Bruce H Lipton, PhD

Spontaneous Evolution: Our positive future by Bruce H Lipton, PhD and Steve Bhaerman

The Force by Stuart Wilde

The Kybalion: Hermetic Philosophy by Three Initiates

The concept of Simple Truths is not connected to any religious or any other cultural philosophy.

The philosophy of Simple Truths is to embrace nature at its finest!

www.SimpleTruthsTheBooks.com